Earthly Cities

Tom Nielsen

Most inhabitants of earthly cities do not know they live in them and call them by their old place names.

Earthly cities are cities for new humans in old habitats.

In earthly cities, the earth interferes with the cities. The earth speaks up.

The inhabitants of earthly cities feel they live on Earth.

Muscle Cities

All the first cities on Earth were built by hand and powered by humans and their livestock.

Settlements were subject to the forces of nature: the direction of the sun, the movement of water and the winds.

Muscle cities were similar to earthly cities in many ways, but far more isolated, with less contact with other cities, and based on a different understanding of 'the earthly'.

Landscapes surrounded the muscle cities. The cities were woven into them.

It was said that air in muscle cities made people free. They dreamt of civil liberties and escaping the bonds of servitude, tribal affiliation and the daily struggle against nature.

Muscle cities accumulated profits from cultivation and trade. Temples, palaces and city gates were the icons of the city. Muscle cities had distinct centres and stood out from the cultivated landscapes and nature.

Almost all muscle cities evolved into machine cities during the 19th and 20th centuries.

Machine Cities

Machine cities were based on extracting resources from the earth and channelling them to urban communities. They first developed where coal-powered machines were invented.

In the machine cities work was done to provide freedom, equality and economic prosperity for their inhabitants. They could also be called the prosperous cities.

Machine cities stretched towards the horizon. Fuelled by the enormous powers of fossil fuel exploitation.

Railways, and later asphalt roads, connected cities to places from which minerals, proteins and carbohydrates could be extracted. Vast hinterlands were deforested, excavated and drained to grow crops and supply the ever-hungry machine cities.

Machine cities were built on the landscape. Where rapid surges towards the horizon made it too expensive or impractical to build, remnants of the landscape were left as the backsides of the cities.

In machine cities, the earth was excavated, utilised and levelled.

The development of machine cities was dependent on the development of standards. Machine cities could also be called standardised cities.

The iconic buildings of machine cities were town halls, railway stations and major industrial companies. Petrol stations lighting up the dark and the smell of gasoline were important to the atmosphere of machine cities.

Life in machine cities was divided between work, leisure and commuting time. Between professions. Between men and women. Between children, adults and old people. Between social classes.

The by-products of machine cities and consumer culture slowly began to haunt the life within them. It gradually became clear that things were not gone just because they were thrown into a river or dug into a hole. That rivers and lakes died if they were used as dumps. That pesticides killed entire ecosystems and not just 'pests' and 'weeds'. The environmental crisis arose as a consequence of life in machine cities.

The first tentative responses to the environmental crisis were anti-urban but still drew on machine metaphors: eco-communities, earthships and autonomous houses. There were dreams of leaving urban civilisation behind to start again outside the modern world and outside cities. A new concept of society, as a place that was social but not urban, was gaining ground.

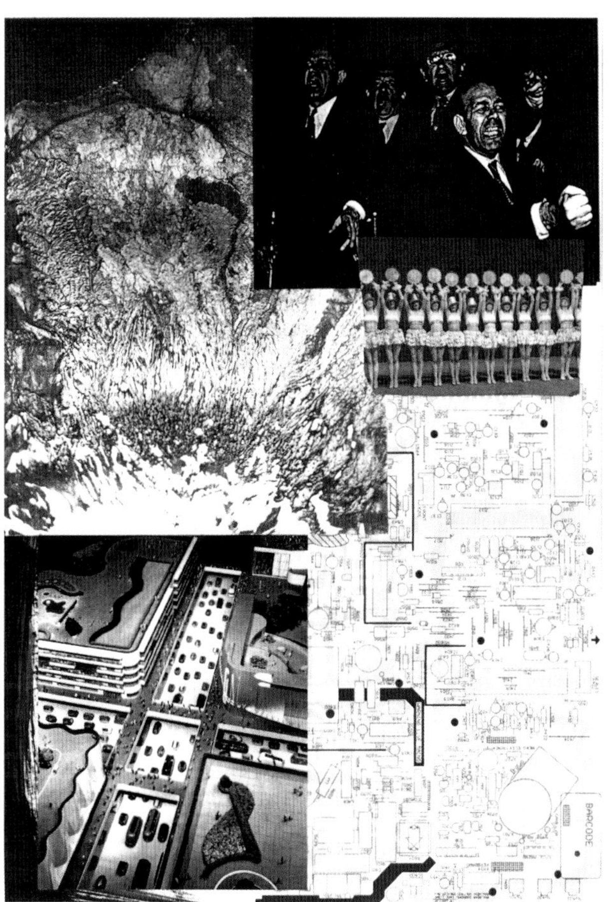

BARCODE

UNION OIL

Cities Without Limits

Cities without limits result from physical and virtual connections enabled by communication technologies and unbridled capital movements.

Cities without limits could also be called global cities because of the real-time connectivity of internet communication between any place on Earth. This created lots of new relationships, required lots of air travel and resulted in lots of physical meetings.

In cities without limits, clear boundaries between cities dissolved. Large and small cities were integrated into urban networks.

Cities without limits are not everywhere, but they could be. Cities without limits are planetary.[1]

Cities without limits exploded into galaxies of larger and smaller urban enclaves, settlements, houses and facilities connected by infrastructure. The dark matter between those bright stars the cities looked like on satellite images made it difficult for people to identify them as cities. The dark matter was very concrete. It was land, often where food was grown. In some places, nature.

The governance of cities without limits became both more local and visible but also more diffuse in transnational and non-localisable networks. A local bakery could be owned by an equity fund no one knew where. The grain used to make the flour in the bread could be grown in fields in another part of the world.

In cities without limits, airports, universities and football stadiums were cathedrals.

The experience of life in cities without limits was characterised by the practice of many residents dividing their activities into portions and distributing them across multiple locations and long distances. 'Thinning' is an important phenomenon in cities without limits.[2] The use of both 'city' and 'countryside' became more fluid, provisional and temporary. Many places have several functions but are not used all the time. Production landscapes can also be leisure landscapes.

It was while living in cities without limits that humans discovered the geological epoch the Anthropocene, anthropogenic climate change and the sixth mass extinction. With cities, we had conquered the Earth. Urbanism had become the dominant way of life on the planet.

It was also while living in cities without limits that the idea of sustainable development was born. The first ideal model of a sustainable city was a compact city.[3]

Densification was a highly symbolic response to the branching and proliferation of cities without limits in a world shaped by a loose market economy and ever-expanding physical and digital communication infrastructures. But in cities without limits, compact and porous parts are two sides of the same coin.

Like the rest of the city without limits, these compact enclaves are based on communication and mobility.

They can be compact because there are other parts that are less compact and where those things that can't happen in the compact parts take place.

The idea of a compact city was driven by a return to a metropolitan concept of urbanism, replacing the suburban dreams of machine cities and filling the gap created by the general lack of understanding of what made cities without limits urban.

The dream of exclusively compact and clearly delimited cities was both unrealistic and impossible at its core but was used as a guiding principle for parts of the urban development. Mayors, strategic planners and urban theorists worked to make the largest cities denser, more compact and higher-performing with one eye closed and the other focused on resource consumption for transport. Contractors, architects, concrete producers, property developers and land sellers in the cities without limits were happy to help with the big task. At the same time, they could also work on building creative and liveable cities. The concentration of as many people as possible within as small an area as possible was a convenient solution.

In the dense, exciting, creative, diverse and affluent parts of the cities without limits, new urbanists now lived in the upgraded, refurbished remnants of machine cities.

The cost of these wonderful urban districts was a gigantic drain on the carbon budget of future generations. It was taken in the hope that future CO_2

savings and moderate transport behaviour within the compact cities would eventually compensate for the squandering it took to build them. Most of those people who moved to urban 'eco-islands' were rich and had a high personal consumption. Not least of second homes and weekend trips around the world. They have not yet started paying off the CO_2 loan in earnest.

Cities without limits don't become earthly just because a small portion of them stop adding to the overall balance sheet.

Even if cities without limits, or the idea of endless resources to power and develop them, do not exist, we will still be living in cities without limits for a long time yet.

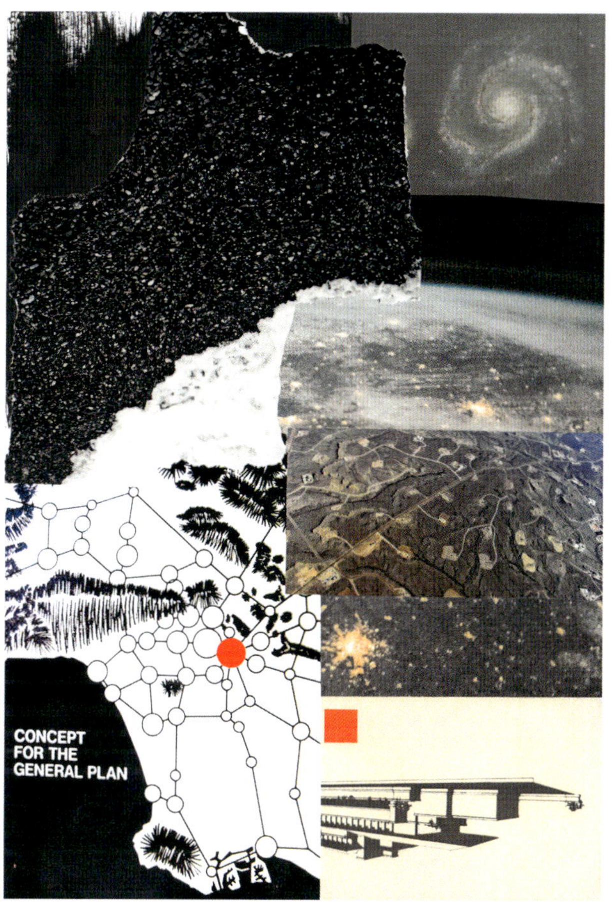
CONCEPT
FOR THE
GENERAL PLAN

Earthly Cities

Earthly cities do not exist. Most people live in machine cities or cities without limits.

Earthly cities emerge through the gradual transformation of cities without limits. There is no unused territory, no virgin land on which to develop earthly cities.

The transition from cities without limits to earthly cities will not be without conflict.

Earthly cities are neither local, national nor global. They are territories. In the words of Bruno Latour, they can be described as 'dwelling places'.[4]

Independence, especially from what was called nature, but also from other people, was a key concept in both machine cities and cities without limits. The eco-utopias inherited this. In earthly cities, dependency is understood as a fact and a central concept. Even a positive value.

In earthly cities, the earth interferes with the cities. The earth speaks up.

Earthly cities will be different all places on Earth.

Earthly cities are landscapes. They can be wet. They can be overgrown. Fog, drought, rain, bloom and harvest are part of the urban experience and a basic condition of urban life.

In earthly cities, the contraction of time and space is less defining of human life and its possibilities than it was in the cities without limits.

Most of the earthly cities were built before they were invented, and earthly cities are never new.

The houses and built structures of earthly cities are inherited and borrowed. The inhabitants look after them and their interests while the world around them changes.

In earthly cities, there is no digging, drilling, piloting or moving earth like there used to be in machine cities and cities without limits.

Earthly cities are not colonial. The extractive logic that was the foundation for machine cities and cities without limits is reversed in earthly cities.

The resources of earthly cities come from themselves, from the earth they are part of, the sun that shines on them, and the water that flows through them. They are organisms with their own metabolism. What is needed to sustain urban life forms is not brought in from the 'land' or 'nature' outside the city – it is found within the cities themselves. This has implications for the understanding of what a city is. Earthly cities are not in a dialectical relationship with the land. Cities are also land and nature.

In earthly cities, the consequences of decisions made by previous civilisations are felt. Areas that were drained and built up as machine cities are flooded. Gases from covered-up, long-forgotten landfills poison the air. The excessive use of asphalt in machine cities and cities without limits makes it hard for earthly cities to breathe.

Earthly cities share their surplus with each other. They are still connected as cities without limits, but their resources are not available to the highest bidder in a global market.

Machine cities and cities without limits were created by the energy from burning fossils from 'underground forests'.[5] In earthly cities, only renewable resources are burned. Unlike the over-energised cities without limits, energy balance is an important goal in earthly cities.

Geology, climate and landscape limit how many resources can be used and conditions what can happen in earthly cities. The form of earthly cities is impacted by resource consumption. Resource mapping is a key activity. Earthly cities can also be called resource cities.

This resource-centricity makes it harder for the inhabitants of earthly cities to take weekend trips to another continent or move goods across the globe than it was for those living in cities without limits.

Earthly cities are the opposite of generic cities,[6] even though most of the things they are made of are mass-produced and found in many places: wind turbines, electric cars, clothes and furniture. The reason they can't be described as generic is because the earthly manifests itself clearly in them. The topography, climate, flora and fauna are not, as in generic cities, merely fragments, backdrops and remnants of what came before them.

The earthly cities have plenty of boundaries and contrasts to be experienced. Wild areas vs. densely built-up areas. Massive stone buildings against light-weight structures. Food production, housing and recreation, all in the same place.

Urbanists in the earthly cities are less concerned with differences in settlement and population density than they were in the cities without limits.

The earthly cities are new versions of the open, fragmented cities that muscle cities evolved into as they became machine cities, and which became open, fragmented and porous on a new scale as network structures in cities without limits.

In the earthly cities, rivers, old trees, food production facilities, energy plants and recycling centres are iconic elements.

There are lots of bikes in earthly cities, wind turbines are city fixtures. Urban trees are not things that can be removed and replaced with new ones. They are as important as ancient monuments and just as cherished as the best, most significant buildings.

There are both orchards and office blocks in most earthly cities.

It is fundamental to earthly cities that the cities without limits they evolve from were already open, full of soil, water and scrub. What is new about the earthly cities is that these elements are considered just as important as the crystalline structures humans have built from concrete, steel, stone and oil materials. The majority of the earthly cities are dominated by natural habitats. Most of them is forest, but fields also take up a lot of space. Most of the food eaten in earthly cities is grown in them.

Rhizome and mycelium are metaphors often used to describe earthly cities. They are more than that. They are synthetic, they are man-made, discontinuous and asymmetrical.

It is impossible to tell where the earthly cities start and end, because they are made up of both built and grown elements, and because they are networks of connected places.

The boundaries of earthly cities are determined by the earthly. Watersheds are important. They can therefore also be called water catchment cities.

Earthly cities are porous.

Water flows through earthly cities, and their waterways are more important than their motorways.

The development of urban islands was one of the problems of urbanism in cities without limits, where the segregation and division into enclaves of wealth, cut off from the rest of the urban population, was destructive. In the earthly cities, physical islands and built-up enclaves will evolve because waterways and wetlands, bio-corridors and topography will ensure a more equal balance between the built and unbuilt. Landscapes soften economic and social boundaries because they are systems that connect across them.

It is hard to distinguish between ecosystems and urban systems in the earthly cities.

Earthly cities are not a loose collection of autonomous houses. Water, wind, electricity, people, animals and plants flow through the buildings and connect them to other buildings in the earthly cities.

The people who live in the houses and the currents that flow through them make them connected. The connected homes show us what kind of cities earthly cities are.

Earthly cities come in all sizes. From a few houses to giant organisms with millions of human inhabitants and an almost infinite number of other living species.

Earthly cities can be both camps and metropolises. Most earthly cities are interconnected networks of smaller settlements, urban districts and large, continuous crystalline urban structures.

Humans are the biggest problem facing earthly cities. Technocrats have long thought that the systems and infrastructures of human habitats would work better without people, or at least without human intervention. Urbanists have never seen it that way before. In the earthly cities, humans must realise that they, their children, neighbours and colleagues, through consumption of food, energy and resources, are the Earth's biggest problem.

Technological developments in earlier urban forms
made cities expand and use more resources. They
created the foundation for the human population
to grow. In the earthly cities, technological developments do the opposite. They help humans help the
Earth against human domination.

The cities without limits were characterised by
deregulation. The earthly cities are regulated so
that there is equal access to Earth's resources for its
inhabitants. The Earth has rights and owns itself.

Spreadsheets are both a blessing and a curse in
earthly cities. They provide an overview of resource
consumption. But they also take away the sense and
experience of the earthly.

Earthly cities are made up of old districts and new
districts that are still being built. They will be based
on both 'primitive' and 'advanced' technologies. It is
the use of all available ideas that makes the earthly
cities use fewer resources and emit less CO_2 than the
cities without limits.

Earthly cities, like the cities without limits, are connected by travel and electronic signals, by physical
and virtual connections. All places contain material,
stories and memories from other places.

Earthly cities are habitats, but not only for humans.
Neither were the muscle cities, the machine cities
nor the cities without limits, but in earthly cities,
the human inhabitants are aware that they live
with other beings. The urban way of life is not only

human. The encounter between strangers means something different in the earthly cities than it did in previous urban forms.

In earthly cities, urbanity is not only related to the intensity of encounters and exchanges between humans but rather the degree of diversity in the experiences and activities humans can have: the extent of entanglements, the amounts of different things to work on and engage in.

Earthly cities are based on a new notion of urbanity that has emerged as the distinction between original and new, natural and artificial, human and biological, culture and nature matters less than it did in previous phases of the urban.

Many things move slower in the earthly cities than they did in the cities without limits. Earthly cities are closely connected. Travelling and communicating between them uses much less energy than travel in cities without limits and therefore is often slower.

Most inhabitants of earthly cities do not know they live in them and call them by their old place names.

Earthly cities are living cities.

Much of what couldn't be accommodated in the attractive compact cities becomes important in the earthly cities. The huge concrete warehouses that were built as a last careless celebration of consumer culture and the decoupling of consumption, production and resource use that characterised the cities without limits. The partially depopulated villages. The large areas of uniform terraced and detached houses which were built in haste after the turn of the millennium as an investment in the future. The suburbs of all times. The station towns. The disused farm buildings. The half-empty industrial areas on the outskirts of cities.

In the earthly cities, people still move around in individual territories but there are meaningful concentrations with denser relationships, just like the central places in hierarchies the planners behind the machine cities thought they could plan. In the earthly cities the relationships are based on watersheds, bioregions, and resource thinking. The movements and relationships are built on the infrastructural networks the earthly cities inherited from the cities without limits.

The hyper-specialised, intense square kilometres of compact urban fabric filled with offices, expensive apartments, theatres, cafés and shopping that, like Manhattan or Jakarta, physically weigh down the ground beneath them are only exceptions in the earthly cities. They are not the goal of urban development. With that, the understanding of urbanity will eventually follow and evolve in the new forms and structures that make up the earthly city. This is possible because agglomeration urbanity and the many different impulses it provided have moved online and become available – in a new diluted and in some ways poorer form – everywhere. There will be little distinction between virtual and real events. Encounters happen in places other than stony cities.

Just like the cities without limits, there will be differences in the degree and direction in which residents of the earthly cities engage. Some will be cosmopolitan; others primarily oriented towards their neighbourhood or home and their loved ones.

Just like in the cities without limits, machine cities and muscle cities, there will be differences between rich and poor, but there will be places where they meet in the earthly cities. In machine cities, the city park and sports stadium were invented for this. In the earthly cities, the need to cooperate around access to locally produced food, drinking water and energy will bring classes together. Unlike the cities without limits, the elite will not be able to choose to consume much more resources than the poor. They have to relate to the territories they inhabit and the limitations that come with it.

Gardeners are an important profession in earthly cities, and many more will be needed than in the cities without limits. Gardeners work with vegetation, especially trees. But gardeners' approach to growth, circularity and adaptation to seasons and climate, to working with nature's processes in a curatorial way, will be important in many other fields. They will be needed as educators, as carers and managers, as city architects and urban planners. Gardeners, like biologists and geologists, will be important advisors in legal disputes.

Cartographers are important in the earthly cities. Citizens will seek ever greater and more accurate knowledge of the Earth they inhabit.

Historians are important in the earthly cities. They remind residents of what life was like before the burning of coal, oil and gas transformed cities.

Questions of preservation, development and the boundaries between them are important in the earthly cities. Therefore, biologists, conservators and restoration architects will work closely with archaeologists, hydrologists and gardeners to determine questions about what can be preserved and what needs to be changed.

Engineers are important in earthly cities because they can show the inhabitants how much energy they can use and how much food to produce. They play an important role in assessing the utility value of materials.

Hydrologists are essential for monitoring and understanding the movement of the different forms of water that surround and flow in the earthly cities.

Lawyers must look after the interests of those who cannot speak for themselves. The earth. Animals, the rivers, the oceans, the mountains.

Architects work together with inhabitants, teachers, psychologists and artists to make earthly cities worth living in. The role of architects in the earthly cities is to combine materials and create spatial connections. They work with the earthly cities as collages.

The atmospheres of earthly cities are important for people to want to develop and live in them. As a meteorological concept: humans depend on maintaining an atmosphere that makes life possible. And as an aesthetic concept: there are an infinite number of aesthetic atmospheres. Many of them will feel different than in the cities without limits.

The atmospheres of the earthly cities are dominated by two things. Firstly, they are afterworlds where people live in the ruins of past civilisations' urban forms. Secondly, they are constantly in the process of becoming. Natural processes are evident and account for the most obvious dynamics that very directly affect the atmospheres. The man-made processes are in dialogue with the natural ones: additions, renovation and demolition. The earthly cities grow, and it is unpredictable what will happen in them.

Earthly cities are messy. Their relationship with the local context varies from place to place and can't be standardised.

Earthly cities are wind-sensitive. Wind can be felt and seen in them. On the moving branches on the many trees or the multiple small and large wind turbines that harvest it as energy.

Earthly cities are sun-orientated. The urban spaces of the earthly cities provide both access to and protection from the sun. The energy of the sun is harvested.

Some earthly cities are dense and intimate like muscle cities with spaces that wrap around the human body. Others are like machine cities or cities without limits with open horizons, and space for different habitats and natures. With monumental elements and structures that cover large areas and are visible from afar.

Earthly cities are soft.[7]

Earthly cities are cities for new humans in old habitats.

There is a greater difference between night and day in earthly cities than in cities without limits.

The inhabitants of earthly cities feel they live on Earth.

BOULEVARD
MORTIE
D'ALGERIE
BOUL. SERURIER
MAC DONALD BOULEVARD SERURIER
BOULEVARD MAC DONALD
CANAL
JAURES
19e
LA CHAPELLE
SAINTE GENIS
L'OURCO
JEAN
AVENUE
PARC DES BUTTES-CHAUMONT
LA VILLETTE
BOUL. DE LA VILLETTE
BOUL. DE BELLEVILLE - BOUL.
16

DAVOUT
SOULT
RUE DES PYRÉNÉES
CHARONNE
COURS DE VINCENNES
ST. MANDÉ
BOULEVARD DE PICPUS
AVENUE DAUMESNIL
DIDEROT
REUILLY
DAUMESNIL
BO DE REUILLY
AVENUE DE
PONIATOWSKI
PORTE DE VINCENNES
LAC DE PICPUS
PORTE DE CHARENTON
BOIS DE VINCENNES
AUTOROUTE DE L'EST
12ᵉ
BERCY
BOULEVARD
QUAI DE BERCY
QUAI DE LA GARE
MASSÉNA
QUAI D'IVRY
AVENUE LYON
QUAI DE LA RAPÉE
QUAI D'AUSTERLITZ
TOLBIAC
SEINE
BOULEVARD DE BASTILLE
BD DE LA BASTILLE
BOULEVARD BOURDON
GRAND CA
VINCENT
AVENUE D'IVRY
13ᵉ
NATIONALE
PORTE D'ITALIE
BOULEVARD CHOISY
AVENUE DE CHOISY
BOULEVARD KELLERMAN
AVENUE D'ITALIE
BOULEVARD AUGUSTE BLANQUI
GOBELINS
AVENUE DES GOBELINS
ARAGO
BOULEVARD ST-JACQUES
BOULEVARD
PARC DE MONTSOURIS
JOURDAN
RENÉ COTY
BOULEVARD RASPAIL
AVENUE LECLERC

1   With the concept of 'Planetary Urbanism', Neil Brenner and Christian Schmid formulated the idea of urbanisation processes that take place at all scales and can no longer be limited to something that can be called cities and is fundamentally different from the countryside, nature or the rural. The idea of planetary urbanism was first formulated by Henri Lefebvre in 1970. See N. Brenner and C. Schmid, 'Planetary urbanisation' in M. Gandey (ed.), *Urban Constellations*, Jovis Berlin 2012, pp. 11–13.

2   The concept of thinning is borrowed from Rem Koolhaas's diagnosis of the relationship between city and countryside in the lecture 'Countryside' held at the Stedelijk Museum, Amsterdam, in 2012. Lecture slides and notes can be found on the website: https://www.oma.com/lectures/countryside

3   Hong Kong was the hero of Newman and Kenworthy's famous graph (1989) on the relationship between petrol consumption and population density. That graph became the image of the first version of the climate-friendly and sustainable city. It was based on an observation about energy consumption but did not include the CO_2 needed to convert low-density cities into ultra-dense cities with metro systems. See R. Ewing, S. Hamidi, G. Tian, D. Proffitt, S. Tonin and L. Fregolent, 'Testing Newman and Kenworthy's Theory of Density and Automobile Dependence', *Journal of Planning Education and Research* 1–16, 2017.

4   See page 87 in Bruno Latour, *Down to Earth: Politics in the New Climatic Regime*. Polity Press 2018. Originally: *Où atterir? Comment s'orienter en politique*. Editions La Découverte, Paris 2017. Latour uses the term 'dwelling places' instead of the word territory, which he finds too closely related to the administrative unit or the state. Addressing the material, physical aspects of urbanism, I prefer using 'territory', in the meaning 'life terrain', as more precise than dwelling place because I can imply a place on Earth that is used and inhabited.

5   The description of the use of fossil fuels such as burning the underground forests is borrowed from Peter Sloterdijk *Prometheus' Remorse. From the Gift of Fire to Global Arson*. Semiotext(e), 2024.

6   Reference is made to Rem Koolhaas's description in 'The Generic City' in OMA, R. Koolhaas, B. Mau, *S, M, L, XL*, The Monacelli Press 1995.

7   The idea of the soft city was formulated by poet Inger
      Christensen in the line 'a city that is soft as a body'
      from Dét (It), Gyldendal 1969 (2019). David Sim unfolds
      the concept as recommendations for an urban design
      practice in *Soft City – Building Density for Everyday Life*,
      Island Press, 2019.

Afterword: Towards an Earthly Urbanism

Urbanism is in crisis and must adapt. First as an understanding of urban life under the new climatic regime. Then as the practice of shaping and managing the development of the city as a living space.

Urbanism emerged as a consequence of industrialisation. This was about understanding the conditions of human life in the new cities. Not just the industrial metropolises, but also the pre-industrial cities that now existed under different conditions.

Throughout the 20th century, urbanism adapted to new realities: class struggle, health issues, migration, the rise of megacities, the development of global capitalism and identity issues. None of these societal challenges have disappeared, nor the crises they triggered, despite the development of models and concepts to understand them and tools to work with them. Now the climate crisis, which itself consists of many different crises, not least the ecological and biodiversity crisis, calls for an urbanist response. Perhaps a true paradigm shift in our understanding of urban life: a new urbanism.

While the other crises have added to and expanded the idea of urbanity as it was developed in the industrial metropolises, the climate crisis and the quest for a more sustainable city may point to something that will more radically change the idea of urbanity: that life in cities and the development of them as habitats must now include living in a broad sense. Since 'urbanism' means 'life form in cities', we will have to rethink the meaning of the term if our interconnectedness and dependence on non-human life forms – flora, fauna, water and soil – is to have consequences. According to Bruno Latour, the 21st century is the age of geo-social questions.[1] This also includes an urbanist question.

Since the machine cities, urbanity has been perceived as something that was mostly found in metropolises. The bigger, the more diverse and densely populated by people, the less characterised by nature and natural processes, the more urban. Smaller cities had less or almost no urbanity. What was labelled as rural – and not just fields with farms, but also towns and villages – was perceived as the opposite of urban.

A concept of nature that is not based on the idea of nature as something other than culture and thus does not see nature as something culture can rely on for energy and resources but as something humans live in balance with changes a lot of things, including the notion of urbanity. While the machine city's understanding of urbanity was centred on agglomeration (leading to the development of both urban and suburban forms of urbanity that were always in dialogue and often in opposition), in earthly cities there is no fundamental opposition between densely built areas and more loosely built ones. The difference lies in the way our relationship to the Earth's ecosystems affects both spaces and life in cities. The most urban places will be where the interaction between systems, between human and non-human inhabitants, is greatest, and the places that are nodes in the different flows through cities.

The communities, and thus the central meeting places in earthly cities, are linked to the shared fate that comes with occupying the same territory. The distribution and optimisation of resources and the cultivation of food, the effort of coordinating and orchestrating the interference of natural systems with human systems require mass meetings, observations at critical points, gathering of food, distribution and allocation of surplus materials and long, troublesome negotiations with non-human neighbours.

Polarisation

The projects and ideas of sustainable cities that developed in the early 21st century as a response to the climate crisis can be described as polarised between techno-optimism and techno-pessimism.[2]

On the one hand, we have the construction industry's (including the architecture industry's) growth-oriented bet that new technology (clean fuel, CO_2-neutral concrete, computer-controlled and -optimised 'smart cities' as an even more efficient version 2.0 of the modernist machine city) will enable a more sustainable and even more potent and transgressive version of the cities without limits that proved unsustainable because life in them exceeded the planet's limits of what it could offer human life. In this version of the sustainable city, transgressions between artificial/natural, living/manufactured, local/regional/global will be increasingly frequent and the distinctions between them increasingly meaningless. This approach can be found in both the old architectural avant-garde of the city without limits and a more technical, engineering-driven part of the profession that sees a techno-optimistic approach as the only realistic way humanity can respond and mitigate the worst consequences of this climate crisis of its own making. The answer here is technological solutions that haven't been developed yet, but which, if worked hard enough, should allow us[3] to continue our comfortable urban lifestyle after all. Bjarke Ingels's mantra 'Hedonistic

Sustainability' can frame this basic attitude; an attitude that can be described as either escapism, pragmatism or optimism.

Opposite this is the hyper-localised, austerity-oriented approach you see in proposals for small transformations and the emphasis on regionality, authenticity, ecology and roots – architectural as well as human and literal. Here, we find a large part of a young avant-garde, students and recent graduates, together with a few hibernating hippies or green converts from the construction industry, all of them working hard to create architecture that does no harm, that is not unfair and that doesn't leave people or animals behind on the platform of a train that, by the way, is travelling exceedingly slowly. Their diligent work results in a lot of small-scale projects: material studies, thatched rammed-earth houses, houses built with extensive use of recycled materials. Landscape architects were first out of the starting blocks and have come the furthest so far: following Ian McHarg's pioneering ideas of 'Design with Nature', landscape urbanism and then the ecological approach was developed. Landscape architecture and planning have taken centre stage with its methods characterised by time, succession and working with both human and non-human actors and elements. When it comes to proposing visions for large urban areas where human housing takes up a lot of space, it quickly becomes harder to see the difference between a landscape-based approach and the development that otherwise takes place as business-as-usual without much thought to the climate crisis.

The latter business-as-usual approach is used for everything that is too big to be realised in rammed earth versions, and where no one wants to pay for sustainability or take responsibility for technological experiments. This applies to most of what is built. Cities are built with the technology and approaches that have characterised construction during the entire era in which global warming and the 6th mass extinction have been known and discussed. The issue has hardly been noticed by parts of the construction industry. Others, perhaps more sympathetic but also hypocritical people tend, after giving talks and formulating strategies on the necessary action in relation to the climate crisis, to shroud their buildings and projects in Excel sheets, outlining compensation strategies and other mental gymnastics that provide theoretical savings on the strain their projects put on the planetary systems.

Down to Earth

What Bruno Latour described in *Down to Earth* (2018 [2017]) as a polarisation between the 'reactionaries' and the 'progressives' can also be seen in the reactions to the climate crisis in construction and urban development. The progressives who, in a constant extension of modernity's idea of emancipation, think about development independently of serious concerns about the resources with which and at whose expense this development and emancipation should take place. The reactionaries, with a more or less stubborn or inspired sense of a wrong speed of change, a wrong ethos or simply a love for the place where they live, cling to the question of identity linked to a place and its historical culture. Somewhere in between but on the same axis are those who don't really *do* anything.

However, according to Latour, none of these positions are appropriate given the intensity with which the Earth has begun to respond to the increasingly efficient and pervasive efforts of humans over centuries to make the globe *our* place. Science suggests that continued modernisation based on the idea of globalisation and an infinite development horizon is impossible, as resources are running out and their extraction and especially their incineration have increasing consequences for life on Earth. Not least for the human habitats: cities. Similarly, the idea of continuing life and the way of inhabiting and cultivating the land that has been going on in places for centuries (even before industrialisation) is impossible as climate change is rapidly altering the conditions for life. This is also what triggers large waves of migration of people who have to find new places to live and thus move in with those who were there first. Latour diagnoses the situation in *Down to Earth*: 'There are no two ways about it: we have to learn to live with the consequences of what we have unleashed,'[4] and 'the planet is much too narrow and limited for the globe of globalization; at the same time, it is too big, infinitely too large, too active, too complex, to remain within the narrow and limited borders of any locality whatsoever.'[5] Or: 'The Global and the Local alike afford us an inadequate purchase on the Terrestrial, which explains the current hopelessness: what can be done about problems at once so large and so small?'[6]

Latour identifies a third, more promising direction for development, which he calls 'the Terrestrial'. In continuation of actor-network thinking, this is about understanding the various actors, human and non-human, as interconnected. The terrestrial includes everything that constitutes the prerequisites for life in what geologists refer to as the 'critical zone', where life takes place between the atmosphere and the bedrock.[7]

Latour's idea of the terrestrial as a horizon of development and what he calls a system of engendering rather than a system of production, as well as his question How can we 'land on Earth?' have received a lot of attention in architecture and design since their publication in 2017. *Down to Earth* is an eye-opening analysis of the problems politics has in responding to the climate crisis. As Latour's analysis suggests, this may be due to the fact that politics uses modern ideas of society, culture and development, and a modern concept of nature. This is the root of the polarisation and confusion between, for example, technological optimism or pessimism that results from the discussion in architectural circles about whether to opt for a 'construction halt' or 'zero-net emission scenarios'. But also, with the denial of climate problems that exist among some of the elite and large parts of the construction industry, and the consequences this has for ever-larger parts of humanity. The former is radically exemplified by the tech elite's construction of luxury bunkers for themselves while preparing for the human exodus to Mars. The latter by the constant construction of homes for a housing market that itself is kept going by the ongoing provision of new products.

A key question that requires development and discussion is what Latour's idea of the terrestrial as development horizon means for the concept of the city and for urbanism. The definition of urbanism has always been linked to modernity, progress and modernisation, even during the adaptations that criticised modernism as architecture and planning practice. A reorientation such as the one Latour proposes towards the terrestrial means that urbanism must be reimagined.

What type of city are we moving towards if we accept Latour's analysis?

The Idea of Earthly Cities

The goal of Latour's text is to address the lack of orientation towards climate issues in the current political debate. The closest Latour gets to a discussion of cities in *Down to Earth*, is to ask the reader to examine the concrete places and landscapes we live and want to live in. In *Down to Earth*, the question of the terrestrial is not an urbanist question.

But it is.

In the later *On the Emergence of an Ecological Class – a Memo* (2022), Bruno Latour and Nikolaj Schultz argued (as Schultz has recently noted[8]) '... for seeing the incipient, possible outlines of an emerging ecological class consisting of those who struggle against the practices of production itself and its destructive consequences, and rally around its collective interests aimed at the preservation of the conditions of habitability. The ecological class thus cuts through what one might call the interests of the old ruling classes – the bourgeoisie, the working class, and to some extent, the peasant class – and unlike these, works in opposition to the logic of production itself.' In continuation, Schultz argues that this also means a lot for the city, which has 'evolved from being a social battleground to being a geo-social battleground'.[9] We cannot think about the development of these living conditions without thinking about the city. It is the cities, entangled as they are with natural processes in hybrid urban landscapes, that are the battleground of the ecological class.

The old conflicts and the aforementioned crises urbanism have to deal with (migration, health, global capitalism, identity issues) are being 'ecologised.' This can already be seen in disputes and discussions around urban development projects, which, according to Schultz, 'unfold as geo-social conflicts between those who want to expand production and those who want to limit it because of its destructive ecological consequences – and where an ecological class struggles to secure the conditions of earthly habitability, both locally and on a planetary scale. Here we see that the geo-social class conflict becomes a conflict about the form of the city itself.'[10]

How can we imagine cities within the framework of a new development trajectory that is not directed towards either the global or the local as two opposites? A trajectory that does not have modernity and its idea of nature as something that lies outside 'society' – and thus also outside cities – as a starting point. And which is not based on an idea of modern development that has infinite resources to develop from? To paraphrase Latour: 'We are terrestrials amid terrestrials' does not lead to the same concept of the city as 'We are humans in nature'.[11]

The city itself, as we know it and have known it for 200 years, is modern. It was created based on the idea that we are humans in nature. Cities are the habitat of the modern emancipated human that has continually grown, through different incarnations and with various setbacks along the way. Does the climate crisis require us to abandon the idea of the city? That seems neither realistic nor meaningful.

Another possibility is to think about the concept and model of the city in relation to the earthly, and try to think about what the discovery of the earthly means as a development horizon for urbanism. Cities where the world we live in and the world we live from (to paraphrase Latour and Schultz in *On the Emergence of an Ecological Class – a Memo*)[12] coincide.

An urbanism which, in Latour's words, is based on 'a view from somewhere' as opposed to the positivist, modern-scientific 'view from nowhere'.

1   Page 63 in Bruno Latour, *Down to Earth: Politics in the New Climatic Regime*. Polity Press 2018. Originally, *Où atterir? Comment s'orienter en politique*. Editions La Découverte, Paris 2017.

2   See for example Rem Koolhaas, 'Advancement versus Apocalypse' in M. Mostafavi and G. Doherty (eds.), *Ecological Urbanism*. Lars Müller Publishers 2010.

3   This 'we' is the privileged part of the population to which I, the majority of Europeans and all the architects and urbanists referred to here belong.

4   Page 20 in *Down to Earth*, op.cit.

5   Page 16 in *Down to Earth*, op.cit.

6   Page 94 in *Down to Earth*, op.cit.

7   Page 78 in *Down to Earth*, op.cit.

8   Nikolaj Schultz, unpublished reply: 'Byen Danmark og de (geo-)sociale konflikter' ("The city of Denmark and the (geo-)social conflicts"), presented at the conference Byen Danmark – hvordan skabes en bæredygtig udvikling, Aarhus School of Architecture, 7 March 2024. Organised by Center for Strategic Urban Research. (Authors translation from Danish to English.)

9   'Byen Danmark og de (geo-)sociale konflikter', op.cit.

10   'Byen Danmark og de (geo-)sociale konflikter', op.cit.

11   'Saying "We are earthbound, we are terrestrials amid terrestrials," does not lead to the same politics as saying "We are humans in nature." The two are not made of the same cloth – or rather of the same mud.' Page 86 in *Down to Earth*, op.cit.

12   Page 41 in Bruno Latour & Nikolaj Schultz, *On the Emergence of an Ecological Class - a Memo*, Polity Press 2022. Originally *Mémo sur la nouvelle classe écologique*, Éditions La Découverte, 2022.

Tom Nielsen
Earthly Cities

1. edition, 1. first print run 2024

© 2024 Danish Architectural Press and Tom Nielsen

Text and illustrations: Tom Nielsen, Aarhus School of Architecture
Editor: Kristoffer Lindhardt Weiss, Danish Architectural Press
Copy-editing/translation: Cornelius Holck Colding
Graphic design: Hans Munk

Printing: Frederiksberg Bogtrykkeri, 2024

ISBN 978-87-7407-055-9

Danish Architectural Press
Copenhagen, Denmark
www.arkitektensforlag.dk